Mastering Generative AI with PyTorch: From

Fundamentals to Advanced Models

Contents

Introduction to Generative AI

What is Generative AI?

Generative AI refers to artificial intelligence models that can create new content. Unlike traditional AI, which focuses on analyzing or predicting based on existing data, generative AI generates new data instances. These models can produce realistic images, text, audio, and even videos, simulating the creativity and productivity typically attributed to humans. The primary goal of generative AI is to learn the underlying patterns in data and use this knowledge to produce novel outputs that are indistinguishable from real data.

Applications of Generative AI

Generative AI has a wide range of applications across various fields:

1. **Art and Design:** AI-generated art is a rapidly growing field, where models create new pieces of visual art, music, and design, often blending styles and concepts.

2. **Healthcare:** In drug discovery, generative models can design new molecules with specific properties, accelerating the development of new medications.

3. **Entertainment:** AI is used to generate realistic characters, scenes, and even entire storylines for video games and movies.

4. **Content Creation:** Automated text generation for articles, reports, and marketing content helps in producing large volumes of text efficiently.

5. **Data Augmentation:** Generative models can create additional training data for machine learning models, improving their performance, especially in scenarios with limited data.

6. **Speech Synthesis:** Generative AI produces human-like speech, which is used in virtual assistants and customer service bots.

Overview of Generative Models

Generative models are designed to generate new data points that are similar to a given training dataset. Key types of generative models include:

1. **Generative Adversarial Networks (GANs):** GANs consist of two neural networks, a generator and a discriminator, that are trained together. The generator creates fake data, while the discriminator tries to distinguish between real and fake data. Over time, the generator improves, producing increasingly realistic data.

2. **Variational Autoencoders (VAEs):** VAEs are probabilistic models that encode input data into a latent space and then decode it back into the original data form. They are particularly useful for generating new data samples similar to the training data.

3. **Autoregressive Models:** These models generate data one step at a time, conditioning each step on the previous ones. Examples include PixelRNN and PixelCNN for images, and GPT for text.

4. **Diffusion Models:** These are probabilistic models that iteratively refine a noisy input to produce a clean output, effectively reversing a diffusion process.

5. **Transformers:** Initially designed for natural language processing, transformers have been adapted for generative tasks, producing coherent and contextually relevant text, images, and more.

Getting Started with PyTorch

Introduction to PyTorch

PyTorch is an open-source machine learning library developed by Facebook's AI Research lab. It is widely used for deep learning applications due to its flexibility, dynamic computation graph, and ease of use. PyTorch provides a rich set of tools for building and training neural networks, making it a popular choice among researchers and practitioners.

Key features of PyTorch:

- **Dynamic Computation Graph:** Unlike static graph frameworks, PyTorch allows for dynamic construction of computation graphs, which is particularly useful for tasks with varying input sizes or structures.

- **Tensor Operations:** PyTorch tensors are similar to NumPy arrays but with additional capabilities, such as running on GPUs for accelerated computation.

- **Autograd:** PyTorch's automatic differentiation library enables easy and efficient calculation of gradients, which is essential for training neural networks.

- **Community and Ecosystem:** A strong community and a growing ecosystem of libraries and tools support PyTorch, including torchvision for vision tasks and torchtext for NLP.

Installing PyTorch

To install PyTorch, you can use pip or conda, depending on your preference and environment. Here's how to install PyTorch using pip:

1. Open your terminal or command prompt.

2. Run the following command to install PyTorch with CUDA support (if you have an NVIDIA GPU and want to leverage it for faster computations):

bash

Copy code

```
pip install torch torchvision torchaudio
```

For systems without CUDA, you can install the CPU-only version:

bash

Copy code

```
pip install torch torchvision torchaudio cpuonly
```

To verify the installation, you can open a Python interpreter and import PyTorch:

python

Copy code

```
import torch print(torch.__version__)
```

This should display the installed version of PyTorch.

Basic PyTorch Operations

PyTorch operations revolve around tensors, which are the fundamental data structures for representing multi-dimensional arrays. Here are some basic operations:

1. **Creating Tensors:**

python

Copy code

```python
import torch # Create a tensor from a list x =
torch.tensor([1, 2, 3, 4]) print(x) # Create a tensor
of zeros = torch.zeros((2, 3)) print(zeros) # Create a
tensor of ones = torch.ones((2, 3)) print(ones) #
Create a random tensor random_tensor =
torch.rand((2, 3)) print(random_tensor)
```

2. **Tensor Operations:**

python

Copy code

```python
# Basic arithmetic y = torch.tensor([5, 6, 7, 8]) z = x
+ y print(z) # Matrix multiplication a =
torch.tensor([[1, 2], [3, 4]]) b = torch.tensor([[5, 6],
```

[7, 8]]) c = torch.matmul(a, b) print(c) # Reshaping tensors reshaped = x.view(2, 2) print(reshaped)

3. **Automatic Differentiation:**

python

Copy code

```
# Define a tensor with gradient tracking x = torch.tensor([1.0, 2.0, 3.0], requires_grad=True) # Perform some operations y = x * 2 + 1 z = y.mean() # Compute gradients z.backward() print(x.grad)
```

Building Your First Neural Network with PyTorch

To build a neural network in PyTorch, you typically use the **torch.nn** module, which provides classes and functions to construct and train neural networks.

Here's a step-by-step guide to building a simple neural network for classifying handwritten digits from the MNIST dataset:

1. **Import Libraries:**

python

Copy code

```
import torch import torch.nn as nn import
torch.optim as optim import torchvision import
torchvision.transforms as transforms
```

2. **Load and Preprocess the Data:**

python

Copy code

```
transform                                    =
transforms.Compose([transforms.ToTensor(),
```

```
transforms.Normalize((0.5,), (0.5,))]) trainset =
torchvision.datasets.MNIST(root='./data', train=True,
download=True, transform=transform) trainloader =
torch.utils.data.DataLoader(trainset, batch_size=64,
shuffle=True) testset =
torchvision.datasets.MNIST(root='./data', train=False,
download=True, transform=transform) testloader =
torch.utils.data.DataLoader(testset, batch_size=64,
shuffle=False)
```

3. **Define the Neural Network:**

python

Copy code

```python
class SimpleNN(nn.Module): def __init__(self):
super(SimpleNN, self).__init__() self.fc1 =
nn.Linear(28 * 28, 128) self.fc2 = nn.Linear(128, 64)
self.fc3 = nn.Linear(64, 10) def forward(self, x): x =
x.view(-1, 28 * 28) x = torch.relu(self.fc1(x)) x =
torch.relu(self.fc2(x)) x = self.fc3(x) return x net =
SimpleNN()
```

4. **Define the Loss Function and Optimizer:**

python

Copy code

```python
criterion = nn.CrossEntropyLoss() optimizer =
optim.SGD(net.parameters(), lr=0.01,
momentum=0.9)
```

5. **Train the Neural Network:**

python

Copy code

```
for epoch in range(5): # loop over the dataset multiple times running_loss = 0.0 for inputs, labels in trainloader: optimizer.zero_grad() # zero the parameter gradients outputs = net(inputs) # forward pass loss = criterion(outputs, labels) # compute loss loss.backward() # backward pass optimizer.step() # optimize the parameters running_loss += loss.item() print(f"Epoch {epoch + 1}, Loss: {running_loss / len(trainloader)}") print("Finished Training")
```

6. **Evaluate the Neural Network:**

python

Copy code

```
correct = 0 total = 0 with torch.no_grad(): for inputs,
labels in testloader: outputs = net(inputs) _,
predicted = torch.max(outputs.data, 1) total +=
labels.size(0) correct += (predicted ==
labels).sum().item() print(f"Accuracy on test set:
{100 * correct / total}%")
```

This completes the process of building, training, and evaluating a simple neural network using PyTorch.

Part II: Generative Models

Generative Adversarial Networks (GANs)

Introduction to GANs

Generative Adversarial Networks (GANs) are a class of machine learning frameworks designed by Ian Goodfellow and his colleagues in 2014. GANs consist of two neural networks, the generator and the discriminator, which compete against each other in a game-theoretic scenario. The generator creates synthetic data resembling the real data, while the discriminator attempts to distinguish between real and fake data. The competition drives both networks to improve their capabilities, resulting in a generator that produces highly realistic data.

Architecture of GANs

The architecture of GANs comprises two main components:

1. **Generator:** The generator is responsible for creating fake data. It takes random noise as input and transforms it into a data instance that mimics the real data. The generator is typically a neural network with several layers that progressively refine the generated output.

2. **Discriminator:** The discriminator's role is to classify inputs as real or fake. It takes data (either from the real dataset or generated by the generator) and outputs a probability score

indicating the likelihood that the data is real. The discriminator is also a neural network, often a convolutional neural network (CNN) in image-related tasks.

The training process involves updating the generator and discriminator iteratively. The generator aims to produce data that maximizes the discriminator's classification error, while the discriminator aims to minimize this error.

Training GANs

Training GANs is a challenging task due to the adversarial nature of the process. The key steps in training GANs are:

1. **Initialize the generator and discriminator networks.**

2. **Train the discriminator:**

   - Feed real data to the discriminator and compute the loss.

   - Feed fake data generated by the generator to the discriminator and compute the loss.

   - Combine these losses and update the discriminator's weights to minimize the loss.

3. **Train the generator:**

   - Generate fake data and pass it through the discriminator.

- Compute the loss based on the discriminator's output.

- Update the generator's weights to maximize the discriminator's loss.

The process is repeated for a number of iterations until the generator produces realistic data.

Implementing GANs with PyTorch

Here's an example of implementing a simple GAN using PyTorch:

1. **Define the Generator and Discriminator Networks:**

python

Copy code

```python
import torch
import torch.nn as nn
import torch.optim as optim

class Generator(nn.Module):
    def __init__(self, input_dim):
        super(Generator, self).__init__()
        self.fc = nn.Sequential(
            nn.Linear(input_dim, 256),
            nn.ReLU(),
            nn.Linear(256, 512),
            nn.ReLU(),
            nn.Linear(512, 1024),
            nn.ReLU(),
            nn.Linear(1024, 28 * 28),
            nn.Tanh()
        )
    def forward(self, x):
        return self.fc(x)

class Discriminator(nn.Module):
    def __init__(self):
        super(Discriminator, self).__init__()
        self.fc = nn.Sequential(
            nn.Linear(28 * 28, 512),
            nn.LeakyReLU(0.2),
            nn.Linear(512, 256),
```

```python
nn.LeakyReLU(0.2), nn.Linear(256, 1), nn.Sigmoid() )

def forward(self, x): return self.fc(x)
```

2. **Training the GAN:**

python

Copy code

```python
import torchvision import torchvision.transforms as
transforms # Hyperparameters lr = 0.0002
batch_size = 64 epochs = 100 z_dim = 100 # Data
Loader transform = transforms.Compose([
transforms.ToTensor(), transforms.Normalize([0.5],
[0.5]) ]) trainset =
torchvision.datasets.MNIST(root='./data', train=True,
download=True, transform=transform) trainloader =
```

```python
torch.utils.data.DataLoader(trainset,

batch_size=batch_size, shuffle=True) # Initialize

networks G = Generator(z_dim) D = Discriminator() #

Loss and optimizers criterion = nn.BCELoss()

optimizer_G = optim.Adam(G.parameters(), lr=lr)

optimizer_D = optim.Adam(D.parameters(), lr=lr) #

Training loop for epoch in range(epochs): for i,

(imgs, _) in enumerate(trainloader): # Train

Discriminator real_imgs = imgs.view(imgs.size(0), -1)

real_labels = torch.ones(imgs.size(0), 1) fake_labels =

torch.zeros(imgs.size(0), 1) # Discriminator loss on

real images outputs = D(real_imgs) d_loss_real =

criterion(outputs, real_labels) # Discriminator loss on
```

```python
# fake images
z = torch.randn(imgs.size(0), z_dim)
fake_imgs = G(z)
outputs = D(fake_imgs)
d_loss_fake = criterion(outputs, fake_labels)
# Total discriminator loss
d_loss = d_loss_real + d_loss_fake
optimizer_D.zero_grad()
d_loss.backward()
optimizer_D.step()
# Train Generator
z = torch.randn(imgs.size(0), z_dim)
fake_imgs = G(z)
outputs = D(fake_imgs)
g_loss = criterion(outputs, real_labels)
optimizer_G.zero_grad()
g_loss.backward()
optimizer_G.step()
print(f'Epoch [{epoch+1}/{epochs}] | d_loss: {d_loss.item():.4f} | g_loss: {g_loss.item():.4f}')
```

Variational Autoencoders (VAEs)

Introduction to VAEs

Variational Autoencoders (VAEs) are a type of generative model that combines neural networks with Bayesian inference. VAEs are particularly effective for generating new data samples and learning latent representations. Unlike traditional autoencoders, which learn a deterministic mapping, VAEs learn a probabilistic mapping from the input space to a latent space, allowing them to generate diverse outputs.

Mathematical Foundations of VAEs

VAEs are built on the principles of variational inference. The key components of VAEs include:

1. **Encoder:** The encoder maps input data to a latent space, producing two outputs: the mean and the standard deviation of a Gaussian distribution.

2. **Latent Space:** A random sample is drawn from the Gaussian distribution parameterized by the encoder's outputs.

3. **Decoder:** The decoder maps the latent sample back to the original data space, reconstructing the input data.

The objective function of VAEs consists of two parts:

1. **Reconstruction Loss:** Measures how well the decoder reconstructs the input data from the latent space.

2. **KL Divergence:** Measures the difference between the learned latent distribution and a prior distribution (typically a standard normal distribution).

The total loss is a combination of these two terms, ensuring that the model learns a useful latent representation while generating realistic data.

Training VAEs

Training VAEs involves minimizing the combined loss function (reconstruction loss + KL divergence). The steps are:

1. **Forward pass through the encoder to get the mean and standard deviation.**

2. **Sample from the Gaussian distribution using the reparameterization trick to ensure backpropagation works.**

3. **Forward pass through the decoder to reconstruct the input.**

4. **Compute the reconstruction loss and KL divergence.**

5. **Backpropagate the loss and update the model parameters.**

Implementing VAEs with PyTorch

Here's an example of implementing a simple VAE using PyTorch:

1. **Define the VAE Network:**

python

Copy code

```python
class VAE(nn.Module):
    def __init__(self, input_dim, hidden_dim, latent_dim):
        super(VAE, self).__init__()
        self.encoder = nn.Sequential(
            nn.Linear(input_dim, hidden_dim),
            nn.ReLU()
        )
        self.fc_mu = nn.Linear(hidden_dim, latent_dim)
        self.fc_logvar = nn.Linear(hidden_dim, latent_dim)
        self.decoder = nn.Sequential(
            nn.Linear(latent_dim, hidden_dim),
            nn.ReLU(),
            nn.Linear(hidden_dim, input_dim),
            nn.Sigmoid()
        )

    def encode(self, x):
        h = self.encoder(x)
        return self.fc_mu(h), self.fc_logvar(h)

    def reparameterize(self, mu, logvar):
        std = torch.exp(0.5 * logvar)
        eps = torch.randn_like(std)
        return mu + eps
```

```python
* std

def decode(self, z):
    return self.decoder(z)

def forward(self, x):
    mu, logvar = self.encode(x)
    z = self.reparameterize(mu, logvar)
    return self.decode(z), mu, logvar

# Loss function
def loss_function(recon_x, x, mu, logvar):
    BCE = nn.functional.binary_cross_entropy(recon_x, x, reduction='sum')
    KLD = -0.5 * torch.sum(1 + logvar - mu.pow(2) - logvar.exp())
    return BCE + KLD
```

2. **Training the VAE:**

python

Copy code

```python
# Hyperparameters
input_dim = 28 * 28
hidden_dim = 400
latent_dim = 20
lr = 0.001
batch_size = 128
```

```python
epochs = 20
# Data Loader
trainset = torchvision.datasets.MNIST(root='./data', train=True, download=True, transform=transforms.ToTensor())
trainloader = torch.utils.data.DataLoader(trainset, batch_size=batch_size, shuffle=True)
# Initialize model and optimizer
vae = VAE(input_dim, hidden_dim, latent_dim)
optimizer = optim.Adam(vae.parameters(), lr=lr)
# Training loop
for epoch in range(epochs):
    train_loss = 0
    for imgs, _ in trainloader:
        imgs = imgs.view(-1, input_dim)
        recon_imgs, mu, logvar = vae(imgs)
        loss = loss_function(recon_imgs, imgs, mu, logvar)
        optimizer.zero_grad()
        loss.backward()
        optimizer.step()
```

```
train_loss += loss.item() print(f'Epoch
[{epoch+1}/{epochs}] | Loss: {train_loss /
len(trainloader.dataset):.4f}')
```

Autoregressive Models

Introduction to Autoregressive Models

Autoregressive models generate data by predicting each element based on the previous elements in a sequence. These models are particularly useful for generating sequential data such as text, audio, and images. They work by modeling the conditional probability of each element given the preceding elements, making them capable of capturing complex dependencies in the data.

Examples: PixelRNN, PixelCNN

1. **PixelRNN:** PixelRNN is an autoregressive model for image generation that uses recurrent neural networks (RNNs) to model the conditional distribution of each pixel given the previous pixels. It processes images row by row, capturing spatial dependencies.

2. **PixelCNN:** PixelCNN is a convolutional variant of PixelRNN, which uses convolutional neural networks (CNNs) to model pixel dependencies. It processes images in a more parallelizable manner compared to PixelRNN, making it more efficient for training and generation.

Both models have been successful in generating high-quality images by effectively capturing the spatial dependencies between pixels.

Implementing Autoregressive Models with PyTorch

Here's an example of implementing a simple autoregressive model for image generation using PyTorch:

1. **Define the PixelCNN Network:**

python

Copy code

```
class PixelCNN(nn.Module): def __init__(self,
input_dim, hidden_dim, output_dim):
super(PixelCNN, self).__init__() self.conv1 =
```

```python
nn.Conv2d(input_dim, hidden_dim, kernel_size=7,
padding=3) self.conv2 = nn.Conv2d(hidden_dim,
hidden_dim, kernel_size=7, padding=3) self.conv3 =
nn.Conv2d(hidden_dim, hidden_dim, kernel_size=7,
padding=3) self.conv4 = nn.Conv2d(hidden_dim,
output_dim, kernel_size=1) self.relu = nn.ReLU() def
forward(self, x): x = self.relu(self.conv1(x)) x =
self.relu(self.conv2(x)) x = self.relu(self.conv3(x)) x =
self.conv4(x) return x # Loss function criterion =
nn.CrossEntropyLoss()
```

2. **Training the PixelCNN:**

python

Copy code

```python
# Hyperparameters input_dim = 1 hidden_dim = 64
output_dim = 256  # Number of possible pixel values
lr = 0.001 batch_size = 64 epochs = 20 # Data Loader
transform           =           transforms.Compose([
transforms.ToTensor(), transforms.Lambda(lambda x:
(x * 255).long()) # Convert to integer pixel values ])
trainset = torchvision.datasets.MNIST(root='./data',
train=True, download=True, transform=transform)
trainloader = torch.utils.data.DataLoader(trainset,
batch_size=batch_size, shuffle=True) # Initialize
model and optimizer pixelcnn = PixelCNN(input_dim,
hidden_dim, output_dim) optimizer =
optim.Adam(pixelcnn.parameters(), lr=lr) # Training
```

```
loop for epoch in range(epochs): train_loss = 0 for
imgs, _ in trainloader: outputs = pixelcnn(imgs)
outputs = outputs.permute(0, 2, 3,
1).contiguous().view(-1, output_dim) # Reshape for
loss computation targets = imgs.view(-1) # Flatten
target images loss = criterion(outputs, targets)
optimizer.zero_grad() loss.backward() optimizer.step()
train_loss += loss.item() print(f'Epoch
[{epoch+1}/{epochs}] | Loss: {train_loss /
len(trainloader.dataset):.4f}')
```

This example demonstrates how to build and train a
PixelCNN model using PyTorch for generating images.
By learning the conditional probabilities of pixels, the

model can generate new images that are similar to the training data.

Generative Adversarial Networks (GANs)

Advanced Topics in GANs

Conditional GANs (cGANs)

Conditional GANs extend the basic GAN framework by conditioning the generator and discriminator on additional information, such as class labels or specific attributes. This allows for more controlled generation of data.

- **Architecture:** The generator and discriminator both receive the conditional information as input. For example, if generating images of specific digits, the digit label is concatenated with the input noise vector for the generator and the input image for the discriminator.

- **Implementation Example:**

python

Copy code

```python
class ConditionalGenerator(nn.Module):
    def __init__(self, input_dim, label_dim):
        super(ConditionalGenerator, self).__init__()
        self.fc = nn.Sequential(
            nn.Linear(input_dim + label_dim, 256),
            nn.ReLU(),
            nn.Linear(256, 512),
            nn.ReLU(),
```

```python
            nn.Linear(512, 1024), nn.ReLU(), nn.Linear(1024, 28
* 28), nn.Tanh() )    def forward(self, x, labels): x =
torch.cat([x, labels], dim=1)    return self.fc(x)    class
ConditionalDiscriminator(nn.Module):                    def
__init__(self,                          label_dim):
super(ConditionalDiscriminator, self).__init__()    self.fc
= nn.Sequential( nn.Linear(28 * 28 + label_dim, 512),
nn.LeakyReLU(0.2),          nn.Linear(512,          256),
nn.LeakyReLU(0.2), nn.Linear(256, 1), nn.Sigmoid() )
def       forward(self,     x,      labels):     x     =
torch.cat([x.view(x.size(0), -1), labels], dim=1)    return
self.fc(x)
```

CycleGANs

CycleGANs enable image-to-image translation without paired examples. For instance, converting images from one domain (e.g., photos) to another (e.g., paintings).

- **Architecture:** Uses two generators and two discriminators. One pair translates from domain A to B, and the other translates back from B to A.
- **Training:** Includes cycle consistency loss, ensuring that translating an image from one domain to another and back yields the original image.

Variational Autoencoders (VAEs)

Advanced Topics in VAEs

Conditional VAEs (cVAEs)

Conditional VAEs introduce conditioning information into the VAE framework, similar to cGANs, for controlled generation.

- **Architecture:** The encoder and decoder are conditioned on additional information, such as class labels.

- **Implementation Example:**

python

Copy code

```
class ConditionalVAE(nn.Module): def __init__(self,
input_dim, hidden_dim, latent_dim, label_dim):
```

```python
super(ConditionalVAE, self).__init__() self.encoder =
nn.Sequential( nn.Linear(input_dim + label_dim,
hidden_dim), nn.ReLU() ) self.fc_mu =
nn.Linear(hidden_dim, latent_dim) self.fc_logvar =
nn.Linear(hidden_dim, latent_dim) self.decoder =
nn.Sequential( nn.Linear(latent_dim + label_dim,
hidden_dim), nn.ReLU(), nn.Linear(hidden_dim,
input_dim), nn.Sigmoid() ) def encode(self, x, labels):
h = self.encoder(torch.cat([x, labels], dim=1)) return
self.fc_mu(h), self.fc_logvar(h) def
reparameterize(self, mu, logvar): std = torch.exp(0.5
* logvar) eps = torch.randn_like(std) return mu + eps
* std def decode(self, z, labels): return
```

```python
self.decoder(torch.cat([z, labels], dim=1)) def

forward(self, x, labels): mu, logvar = self.encode(x,

labels) z = self.reparameterize(mu, logvar) return

self.decode(z, labels), mu, logvar
```

Autoregressive Models

Advanced Topics in Autoregressive Models

Attention Mechanisms

Attention mechanisms allow models to focus on relevant parts of the input sequence when making predictions, significantly improving the performance of autoregressive models in tasks like machine translation and image generation.

Transformers

Transformers use self-attention mechanisms to process sequential data in parallel, which enhances efficiency and performance in tasks such as language modeling and text generation.

Generative Models with PyTorch

Implementing Conditional GANs with PyTorch

1. **Data Preparation:**

python

Copy code

```python
# Assuming labels are available in the dataset trainset

= torchvision.datasets.MNIST(root='./data',

train=True, download=True, transform=transform)

trainloader = torch.utils.data.DataLoader(trainset,

batch_size=batch_size, shuffle=True)
```

2. **Training Conditional GAN:**

python

Copy code

```python
# Label embedding for conditional input num_classes

= 10 label_dim = num_classes def one_hot(labels,

num_classes): return torch.eye(num_classes)[labels]
```

```python
for epoch in range(epochs): for imgs, labels in
trainloader: real_imgs = imgs.view(imgs.size(0), -1)
real_labels = one_hot(labels, num_classes)
fake_labels = one_hot(torch.randint(0, num_classes,
(imgs.size(0),)), num_classes) # Train Discriminator
real_outputs = D(real_imgs, real_labels) d_loss_real =
criterion(real_outputs, torch.ones(imgs.size(0), 1)) z
= torch.randn(imgs.size(0), z_dim) fake_imgs = G(z,
fake_labels) fake_outputs = D(fake_imgs, fake_labels)
d_loss_fake = criterion(fake_outputs,
torch.zeros(imgs.size(0), 1)) d_loss = d_loss_real +
d_loss_fake optimizer_D.zero_grad()
d_loss.backward() optimizer_D.step() # Train
```

```python
Generator z = torch.randn(imgs.size(0), z_dim)
fake_imgs = G(z, fake_labels) outputs = D(fake_imgs,
fake_labels) g_loss = criterion(outputs,
torch.ones(imgs.size(0), 1)) optimizer_G.zero_grad()
g_loss.backward() optimizer_G.step() print(f'Epoch
[{epoch+1}/{epochs}] | d_loss: {d_loss.item():.4f} |
g_loss: {g_loss.item():.4f}')
```

Summary

In this section, we explored advanced generative models, including GANs, VAEs, and autoregressive models, and demonstrated how to implement them using PyTorch. These models enable the creation of realistic synthetic data, conditional data generation, and image-to-image translation, showcasing the versatility and power of generative AI.

Implementing Variational Autoencoders (VAEs) with PyTorch

1. **Data Preparation:**

Ensure the dataset is loaded and preprocessed:

python

Copy code

```python
# Data Loader transform = transforms.Compose([
transforms.ToTensor(), transforms.Lambda(lambda x:
x.view(-1)) # Flatten the image ]) trainset =
torchvision.datasets.MNIST(root='./data', train=True,
download=True, transform=transform) trainloader =
torch.utils.data.DataLoader(trainset,
batch_size=batch_size, shuffle=True)
```

2. Training the VAE:

The training loop for a VAE involves computing the reconstruction loss and the KL divergence:

python

Copy code

```python
# Hyperparameters
input_dim = 28 * 28
hidden_dim = 400
latent_dim = 20
lr = 0.001
batch_size = 128
epochs = 20
# Initialize model and optimizer
vae = VAE(input_dim, hidden_dim, latent_dim)
optimizer = optim.Adam(vae.parameters(), lr=lr)
# Training loop
for epoch in range(epochs):
    train_loss = 0
    for imgs, _ in trainloader:
        imgs = imgs.view(-1, input_dim)
        recon_imgs, mu, logvar = vae(imgs)
        loss = loss_function(recon_imgs, imgs, mu, logvar)
        optimizer.zero_grad()
        loss.backward()
        optimizer.step()
        train_loss += loss.item()
    print(f'Epoch [{epoch+1}/{epochs}] | Loss: {train_loss / len(trainloader.dataset):.4f}')
```

Implementing Autoregressive Models with PyTorch

1. Data Preparation:

For autoregressive models, the data needs to be prepared so that each element can be predicted based on previous elements:

python

Copy code

```
# Data Loader with integer pixel values transform =
transforms.Compose([           transforms.ToTensor(),
transforms.Lambda(lambda  x:  (x  *  255).long())  #
Convert  to  integer  pixel  values  ])  trainset  =
torchvision.datasets.MNIST(root='./data', train=True,
download=True, transform=transform) trainloader =
```

```
torch.utils.data.DataLoader(trainset,

batch_size=batch_size, shuffle=True)
```

2. **Training the PixelCNN:**

The training loop for PixelCNN involves computing the loss for each pixel and updating the model parameters:

python

Copy code

```
# Hyperparameters input_dim = 1 hidden_dim = 64

output_dim = 256  # Number of possible pixel values

lr = 0.001 batch_size = 64 epochs = 20 # Initialize

model and optimizer pixelcnn = PixelCNN(input_dim,

hidden_dim,      output_dim)      optimizer      =

optim.Adam(pixelcnn.parameters(), lr=lr) # Training
```

```python
loop for epoch in range(epochs): train_loss = 0 for
imgs, _ in trainloader: outputs = pixelcnn(imgs)
outputs = outputs.permute(0, 2, 3,
1).contiguous().view(-1, output_dim) # Reshape for
loss computation targets = imgs.view(-1) # Flatten
target images loss = criterion(outputs, targets)
optimizer.zero_grad() loss.backward() optimizer.step()
train_loss += loss.item() print(f'Epoch
[{epoch+1}/{epochs}] | Loss: {train_loss /
len(trainloader.dataset):.4f}')
```

Summary and Next Steps

In this section, we covered the implementation of
several generative models using PyTorch:

1. **Generative Adversarial Networks (GANs):** We discussed the basics of GANs, their architecture, and training process. We also touched on advanced GANs such as Conditional GANs and CycleGANs, which allow for more controlled and diverse data generation.

2. **Variational Autoencoders (VAEs):** We explored VAEs, their mathematical foundations, and how to implement them. Conditional VAEs (cVAEs) were also introduced for generating data conditioned on additional information.

3. **Autoregressive Models:** We examined autoregressive models like PixelCNN, their applications in sequential data generation, and

the use of attention mechanisms and transformers for enhancing performance.

Each of these models has unique strengths and can be applied to various tasks in generative AI. By understanding their architectures and training processes, you can leverage these models to create realistic and diverse data for a wide range of applications.

Building Efficient Data Pipelines for Generative AI in PyTorch

The effectiveness of any generative AI model hinges not only on its architecture but also on the quality and efficiency of its data pipeline. PyTorch provides extensive tools and utilities to streamline the process of loading, preprocessing, and augmenting data for training and evaluation. This chapter delves into the design and implementation of advanced data pipelines tailored for generative AI tasks, ensuring optimal utilization of resources and enhanced model performance.

A data pipeline is the backbone of machine learning workflows. For generative models, such pipelines must handle large-scale datasets, often requiring intricate preprocessing steps to format data appropriately. In computer vision, this could mean resizing images, applying transformations, and normalizing pixel values. For natural language processing (NLP), tokenizing text, handling out-of-vocabulary words, and preparing sequences for model consumption are typical steps. PyTorch's modular design, especially with torch.utils.data and torchvision.transforms, provides a foundation to address these challenges.

One of the most crucial steps in building a generative model is understanding your data's structure and variability. Let's consider a scenario where we are developing a text-to-image model. Here, the pipeline must not only load text and corresponding image pairs but also ensure that the data representations are aligned. For example, a caption describing a scenic view must be paired with its corresponding image during training. Misalignment in data could lead to degraded performance and increased training time.

To achieve this alignment, PyTorch's Dataset and DataLoader classes come into play. The Dataset class is designed to load and process individual samples, while the DataLoader handles batch processing and parallel loading. For instance:

python

Copy code

```python
import torch

from torch.utils.data import Dataset, DataLoader

from torchvision import transforms

from PIL import Image


class TextImageDataset(Dataset):
```

```python
def __init__(self, annotations_file, img_dir, transform=None):
    self.img_labels = pd.read_csv(annotations_file)
    self.img_dir = img_dir
    self.transform = transform


def __len__(self):
    return len(self.img_labels)


def __getitem__(self, idx):
    img_path = os.path.join(self.img_dir, self.img_labels.iloc[idx, 0])
    image = Image.open(img_path).convert("RGB")
    caption = self.img_labels.iloc[idx, 1]
    if self.transform:
```

```python
        image = self.transform(image)

        return image, caption


transform = transforms.Compose([

    transforms.Resize((128, 128)),

    transforms.ToTensor(),

    transforms.Normalize((0.5,), (0.5,))

])


dataset = TextImageDataset('annotations.csv',

'images/', transform=transform)

dataloader = DataLoader(dataset, batch_size=32,

shuffle=True)
```

The flexibility of this setup allows custom transformations and efficient data augmentation. Augmentation strategies like flipping, rotation, and cropping are essential in improving the robustness of generative models. Moreover, for text data, techniques like synonym replacement or back-translation can be used.

Another advanced concept is the incorporation of on-the-fly data generation. For some tasks, preloading large datasets may not be feasible due to memory constraints. Instead, generating data during training can be advantageous. PyTorch supports this through its generator functions. For example, in GANs

(Generative Adversarial Networks), synthetic data samples can be generated at runtime and fed into the discriminator for training.

Consider a GAN training scenario where the generator synthesizes fake images, and these images are combined with real ones to train the discriminator. Here's an outline:

python

Copy code

```
for real_images, _ in dataloader:
    noise = torch.randn(batch_size, latent_dim, 1, 1).to(device)
    fake_images = generator(noise)
```

```
# Train discriminator on real and fake images

real_preds = discriminator(real_images)

fake_preds = discriminator(fake_images.detach())


# Compute loss and update

d_loss = loss_fn(real_preds, real_labels) +

loss_fn(fake_preds, fake_labels)

d_optimizer.zero_grad()

d_loss.backward()

d_optimizer.step()
```

In this example, the noise vector serves as a dynamic

input, reducing the need for pre-computed datasets

while allowing endless variations in the training data.

Scalability is another critical aspect of generative AI pipelines. Leveraging multiple GPUs or distributed environments can drastically reduce training time. PyTorch's torch.nn.DataParallel and torch.distributed modules facilitate this process. By splitting batches across devices and synchronizing gradients, these tools ensure efficient utilization of hardware.

```python
Copy code
model = torch.nn.DataParallel(generator).to(device)


for epoch in range(num_epochs):
    for batch in dataloader:
        optimizer.zero_grad()
```

```
output = model(batch)

loss = loss_fn(output, target)

loss.backward()

optimizer.step()
```

For extreme scalability, consider integrating PyTorch with libraries like Horovod or PyTorch Lightning. These frameworks simplify distributed training and manage underlying complexities like gradient synchronization and checkpointing.

Finally, optimizing the data pipeline for I/O performance is often overlooked but critical for maximizing throughput. Utilizing PyTorch's built-in prefetch_factor and num_workers parameters in the

DataLoader allows asynchronous data loading, reducing bottlenecks.

python

Copy code

```python
dataloader = DataLoader(
    dataset,
    batch_size=64,
    shuffle=True,
    num_workers=4,
    prefetch_factor=2
)
```

Such configurations, combined with efficient file formats like TFRecord or HDF5, can significantly boost performance. Additionally, tools like NVIDIA DALI offer accelerated data pipelines by offloading preprocessing tasks to the GPU.

Advanced Techniques in Training Generative Models with PyTorch

Training generative models presents unique challenges, from ensuring stability in adversarial training to optimizing the balance between creativity and realism in the output. This chapter dives into advanced techniques for training generative models in PyTorch, exploring methods for improving model convergence, handling overfitting, and incorporating advanced loss functions that provide more nuanced feedback to the model during training.

Stabilizing GAN Training

Generative Adversarial Networks (GANs) are notorious for their instability during training. The game-theoretic nature of the adversarial process – where the generator and discriminator compete – often leads to issues such as mode collapse, vanishing gradients, and non-convergence. Several advanced techniques can help address these problems.

One common approach is the use of **Wasserstein GANs** (WGAN), which introduces a new loss function to improve training stability by using the Earth Mover's (Wasserstein) distance between the real and generated data distributions. WGAN eliminates the need for a sigmoid output on the discriminator (now called the critic) and uses weight clipping or gradient

penalty to enforce a Lipschitz constraint, ensuring

more stable gradients.

python

Copy code

```python
# Wasserstein GAN implementation
def discriminator_loss(real_output, fake_output):
    return torch.mean(fake_output) -
torch.mean(real_output)


def generator_loss(fake_output):
    return -torch.mean(fake_output)
```

Another approach is the use of **Least Squares GANs**

(LSGAN), which modifies the loss function to use least

squares error instead of binary cross-entropy. This adjustment helps in avoiding vanishing gradients and ensures that the generator and discriminator feedback is more informative, allowing the model to converge faster and produce higher-quality samples.

python

Copy code

```python
# Least Squares GAN implementation
def discriminator_loss_d(real_output, fake_output):
    return 0.5 * torch.mean((real_output - 1) ** 2 + fake_output ** 2)


def generator_loss_g(fake_output):
    return 0.5 * torch.mean((fake_output - 1) ** 2)
```

Both techniques help mitigate the instability issues traditionally associated with GANs, allowing for smoother and more efficient training.

Improving Convergence with Progressive Growing

Progressive Growing of GANs (PGGAN) is another advanced technique for stabilizing training, especially when generating high-resolution images. Instead of training the GAN on the full resolution from the beginning, PGGAN starts by training the model on low-resolution images and progressively increases the image resolution as the model stabilizes.

python

Copy code

```
# Example of progressive growing strategy
```

```python
class ProgressiveGrowingGenerator(nn.Module):

    def __init__(self, start_resolution=4,
max_resolution=128):

        super(ProgressiveGrowingGenerator,
self).__init__()

        self.start_resolution = start_resolution

        self.max_resolution = max_resolution

        # Define layers here


    def forward(self, z, resolution):

        # Select the appropriate layer based on current
resolution

        pass
```

This technique significantly reduces training time for high-resolution image generation and prevents mode collapse, where the generator produces the same output repeatedly. The gradual increase in resolution allows the model to focus on coarse details first and refine them progressively.

Adversarial Regularization Techniques

In addition to using advanced loss functions, regularization methods are essential for improving the generalization of generative models. For instance, **spectral normalization** has become a popular technique to stabilize the training of GANs. It normalizes the weights of the discriminator by controlling the spectral norm, which prevents the discriminator from becoming too powerful compared to the generator. Spectral normalization works by dividing the weight matrix by its largest singular value.

python

Copy code

```python
# Spectral Normalization on the Discriminator layer
class SpectralNorm(nn.Module):
    def __init__(self, layer):
        super(SpectralNorm, self).__init__()
        self.layer = layer
        self.layer = spectral_norm(self.layer)

    def forward(self, x):
        return self.layer(x)
```

Incorporating such regularization techniques helps

maintain a healthy competition between the

generator and the discriminator, ensuring that the

generator doesn't overpower the discriminator or vice

versa.

Hyperparameter Optimization for Generative Models

Hyperparameter tuning is crucial in achieving the best

possible performance for generative models. In

generative AI, hyperparameters play an even more

significant role due to the inherent complexity and

variability of the models. This chapter will explore

how to efficiently perform hyperparameter

optimization and the strategies you can employ to

discover the optimal set of parameters for your generative models.

Understanding Key Hyperparameters in Generative Models

The success of generative models like GANs, Variational Autoencoders (VAEs), or Diffusion Models largely depends on the right selection of hyperparameters. Some critical parameters include:

- **Learning Rate**: The learning rate controls the step size during optimization. A learning rate that's too high may cause the model to overshoot the optimal weights, while a rate that's too low can make convergence slow.

- **Batch Size**: Larger batches provide more stable estimates of the gradient but may consume more memory. Smaller batches introduce more variance, which can sometimes help avoid local minima.

- **Latent Dimension**: In GANs or VAEs, the latent space dimensionality determines the complexity and diversity of generated samples. Too small a latent space might lead to overfitting, while too large a space could introduce noise.

Grid Search and Random Search

Grid search and random search are the most straightforward methods of hyperparameter optimization. In grid search, you define a range of values for each hyperparameter and exhaustively

search through all combinations. While exhaustive,

grid search can be computationally expensive.

Random search, on the other hand, samples random

combinations from the hyperparameter space and

often finds good configurations faster than grid search.

python

Copy code

```python
from sklearn.model_selection import
RandomizedSearchCV
# Example of Random Search for GAN
param_distributions = {'lr': [0.0001, 0.0005, 0.001],
'batch_size': [16, 32, 64]}
```

```
random_search =

RandomizedSearchCV(estimator=model,

param_distributions=param_distributions, n_iter=10)
```

While grid search guarantees that all possibilities are considered, random search typically converges more quickly to an optimal or near-optimal set of hyperparameters, especially in high-dimensional spaces.

Bayesian Optimization

Bayesian optimization is a more advanced technique that models the function being optimized and tries to find the global optimum with fewer evaluations. By using probabilistic models to predict the next most promising set of hyperparameters based on previous evaluations, Bayesian optimization reduces the number of required trials significantly.

python

Copy code

```python
from skopt import BayesSearchCV
# Example of Bayesian Optimization
opt = BayesSearchCV(model, {'lr': (1e-6, 1e-2, 'log-uniform')}, n_iter=50)
opt.fit(X, y)
```

Automated Machine Learning (AutoML)

AutoML frameworks like Optuna and Ray Tune automate the process of hyperparameter tuning by implementing advanced optimization techniques, such as evolutionary algorithms and multi-fidelity optimization. These frameworks provide user-friendly interfaces and can dramatically speed up the tuning process.

python

Copy code

```python
import optuna

def objective(trial):
    lr = trial.suggest_loguniform('lr', 1e-5, 1e-1)
    batch_size = trial.suggest_categorical('batch_size', [16, 32, 64])
    model = MyModel(lr=lr, batch_size=batch_size)
    # Train model and return validation loss
    return validation_loss
```

AutoML not only speeds up hyperparameter optimization but also assists in automating the selection of the most suitable model architecture for a given task.

Incorporating Transfer Learning in Generative AI

Transfer learning has revolutionized many aspects of deep learning, especially in computer vision and natural language processing. The idea behind transfer learning is to leverage pre-trained models on large datasets and fine-tune them for a specific task. This chapter will explore how to integrate transfer learning techniques into generative models using PyTorch, enabling faster convergence and better generalization.

Pre-trained Models for Generative Tasks

Many generative tasks can benefit from the knowledge embedded in pre-trained models. For instance, in text generation tasks, a pre-trained transformer like GPT-3 or T5 can be used as the base model, and then fine-tuned on specific tasks like story generation or dialogue systems. Similarly, in image generation tasks, a model pre-trained on ImageNet can be leveraged and fine-tuned for tasks like super-resolution or style transfer.

Using PyTorch, you can easily load pre-trained models from torchvision.models for vision tasks or transformers for NLP tasks.

python

Copy code

```
from torchvision import models

resnet18 = models.resnet18(pretrained=True)


# Modify the final layer for the new task

resnet18.fc = nn.Linear(resnet18.fc.in_features,

num_classes)
```

For generative tasks like GANs, pre-trained discriminators can be used to speed up training. This strategy is particularly useful in settings where labeled data is sparse but large amounts of unlabelled data are available.

Fine-tuning Pre-trained Generative Models

Fine-tuning involves adjusting the weights of a pre-trained model slightly for a new task while retaining most of the learned features. This is particularly effective in generative models, where the general features learned during pre-training (e.g., texture, shapes, and object patterns in GANs) can be adapted to a more specific domain with minimal data.

python

Copy code

```python
# Fine-tuning a pre-trained generator for a specific domain
class FineTunedGenerator(nn.Module):
    def __init__(self, pretrained_generator):
        super(FineTunedGenerator, self).__init__()
```

```python
        self.generator = pretrained_generator

        # Modify layers for the specific task


    def forward(self, z):

        return self.generator(z)
```

Fine-tuning generative models has shown significant improvements in reducing the amount of training data required while also leading to higher-quality outputs, especially in domains where high-quality, domain-specific data is scarce.

Optimizing Generative Models with Reinforcement Learning

Reinforcement Learning (RL) offers a powerful way to optimize generative models, particularly when the output of the model needs to satisfy a specific criterion that cannot easily be expressed with a traditional loss function. This chapter explores how to use RL in generative modeling, enabling models to learn from their interactions with the environment or based on user feedback.

Reinforcement Learning for Image Generation

In image generation, RL can be used to guide the generation process toward specific goals. For example, an agent can generate images and receive rewards based on how closely the image matches a desired outcome, such as realistic texture or style.

The policy gradient methods, like Proximal Policy Optimization (PPO), have been used to train generative models in an RL setting. Here's a simple RL setup in PyTorch that demonstrates policy-based optimization for generating an image:

python

Copy code

```python
# RL agent generating an image
class RLImageGenerator(nn.Module):
    def __init__(self):
        super(RLImageGenerator, self).__init__()
        self.generator = Generator()
        self.optimizer = optim.Adam(self.generator.parameters(), lr=0.001)
```

```python
def forward(self, z):

    return self.generator(z)


def update(self, rewards):

    # Update model based on the rewards

    loss = compute_loss(rewards)

    self.optimizer.zero_grad()

    loss.backward()

    self.optimizer.step()
```

RL enables models to optimize for more complex, higher-level objectives, providing flexibility in terms of output quality.

1. Case Study: Fine-Tuning a Language Model for Healthcare Applications

Overview:

- Context: Leveraging GPT-like models for medical transcription and diagnosis recommendations.

- Goal: Develop a domain-specific fine-tuned language model to improve healthcare accessibility.

Key Points:

- **Problem Statement**: Generic LLMs struggle with medical jargon, causing inaccuracies.

- **Solution**: Fine-tune an LLM on a curated dataset of medical literature, patient records (anonymized), and research articles.

- **Challenges**:
  - Data privacy and compliance (HIPAA).
  - Ensuring balanced datasets to prevent biases.

- **Implementation**:
  - Preprocessing data for tokenization, removing redundant information.
  - Domain-specific evaluation using BLEU scores for summaries and clinical relevance tests.

- **Outcomes**:

- Improved accuracy in medical text summarization and diagnoses suggestions.
- Time and cost savings for physicians.

2. Case Study: Scaling a Customer Support Chatbot with Generative AI

Overview:

- Context: An e-commerce platform seeking to automate customer queries.

- Goal: Deploy a scalable chatbot to handle over 70% of customer support inquiries.

Key Points:

- **Problem Statement**: Existing systems relied heavily on keyword-based responses, failing in nuanced contexts.

- **Solution**: Use a fine-tuned conversational LLM integrated with the company's support knowledge base.

- **Challenges**:

  o Handling scalability during seasonal spikes.

  o Maintaining consistent tone and accuracy.

- **Implementation**:

  o Data preparation: Integrating historical customer queries and agent responses.

  o Model optimization for cost-efficiency using AWS Inferentia hardware.

- Deploying and monitoring via a CI/CD pipeline.

- **Outcomes**:

    - 85% accuracy in first-response resolution.

    - Reduced dependency on human agents by 60%.

3. Case Study: Training a Multimodal Model for Retail Recommendations

Overview:

- Context: Improving product recommendations by combining text and image data.

- Goal: Build a multimodal model that enhances customer shopping experiences.

Key Points:

- **Problem Statement**: Text-based recommendation engines overlooked visual elements like style or aesthetics.

- **Solution**: Train a multimodal model using textual product descriptions and corresponding images.

- **Challenges**:

  - Synchronizing text and image embeddings.

  - Ensuring balanced representation of product categories.

- **Implementation**:

  - Framework: PyTorch with HuggingFace Transformers and vision models like CLIP.

  - Data augmentation for skewed product categories.

- Model fine-tuning for cross-modal alignment.

- **Outcomes**:

    - Significant increase in click-through rates (CTR).

    - Enhanced user engagement on the platform.

4. Case Study: Building a Generative Model for Personalized Marketing

Overview:

- Context: A travel company aiming to enhance personalized communication.

- Goal: Generate tailored email campaigns based on customer preferences.

Key Points:

- **Problem Statement**: Current marketing systems lacked personalization, leading to reduced engagement rates.

- **Solution**: Train a generative LLM on customer segmentation data and travel trends.

- **Challenges**:

  - Avoiding generic output by fine-tuning on customer-specific features.

  - Ensuring output remains engaging and aligns with the company's brand.

- **Implementation**:

- Dataset creation: Extract customer preferences, destinations, and seasonal interests.

- Model training: Use a decoder-based architecture for creative text generation.

- Evaluation: Conduct A/B testing on engagement metrics.

- **Outcomes**:

  - Open rates increased by 25%, and click rates by 15%.

  - Enhanced customer satisfaction and retention.

5. Case Study: Implementing Ethical AI Practices in a Financial Institution

Overview:

- Context: A global bank adopting generative AI for fraud detection.

- Goal: Build a model that maintains transparency and fairness in financial decisions.

Key Points:

- **Problem Statement**: AI models in finance are often opaque, risking regulatory scrutiny and public trust.
- **Solution**: Deploy explainable LLMs for fraud analysis and risk assessment.
- **Challenges**:
  - Addressing biases in historical financial data.
  - Complying with financial regulations.
- **Implementation**:

- Data preprocessing: Removing biased transactions and ensuring demographic representation.

- Model training: Focus on interpretability techniques like SHAP values.

- Monitoring: Real-time tracking of false positives/negatives.

- **Outcomes**:

  - Enhanced detection of fraudulent transactions with minimal bias.

  - Compliance with regulatory guidelines and increased stakeholder trust.

6. Case Study: Optimizing a Generative Model for Real-Time Language Translation

Overview:

- **Context**: A global education company aiming to provide real-time language translation for online courses.

- **Goal**: Deploy a low-latency generative model for translating educational content into multiple languages.

Key Points:

- **Problem Statement**: Standard translation models struggled with context in technical content, leading to inaccuracies.
- **Solution**: Fine-tune a pre-trained LLM (e.g., T5 or MarianMT) on domain-specific datasets containing technical jargon and colloquial usage.
- **Challenges**:
    - Reducing inference time while maintaining translation quality.

- Handling code-mixed sentences (language switching mid-sentence).
- Aligning translations with cultural nuances.

- **Implementation**:

1. **Data Preparation**:

   - Gathered multilingual datasets from course content, subtitles, and instructor-provided glossaries.
   - Used preprocessing techniques to remove irrelevant metadata.

2. **Model Training**:

   - Initialized with pre-trained weights from a multilingual model.

- Fine-tuned using cross-entropy loss with custom metrics like BLEU and METEOR for evaluation.

3. **Optimization**:

   - Deployed the model using ONNX Runtime for optimized performance.

   - Leveraged batch processing and beam search for efficient translation.

4. **Monitoring and Feedback**:

   - Incorporated user feedback to improve rare language pairs.

- **Outcomes**:

   - Achieved 98% accuracy for technical terms and idiomatic phrases.

- Reduced latency by 40%, enabling real-time classroom interactions.

- Increased student satisfaction scores across multilingual cohorts.

---

7. Case Study: Developing a Generative Art Application with LLM and Stable Diffusion

Overview:

- **Context**: A creative agency wanted to automate the generation of custom art for branding campaigns.

- **Goal**: Build an application integrating text-to-image capabilities using an LLM and Stable Diffusion.

Key Points:

- **Problem Statement**: Manual design processes were slow and unable to scale for demand.
- **Solution**: Create a pipeline where users provide text prompts describing desired art styles and themes, generating images dynamically.
- **Challenges**:
  - Balancing artistic creativity with client-specific constraints.
  - Ensuring high-resolution outputs suitable for print and digital media.

- Preventing misuse or generation of inappropriate content.

- **Implementation**:

1. **Pipeline Design**:

    - Combined GPT-4 for prompt engineering and Stable Diffusion for image generation.

    - Allowed users to iteratively refine prompts via a conversational interface.

2. **Training and Fine-Tuning**:

    - Fine-tuned Stable Diffusion on a custom dataset of branding and advertising visuals.

- Incorporated LLM-guided content moderation to prevent policy violations.

3. **Infrastructure**:

   - Used GPU instances on AWS for training and inference.
   - Developed a user-friendly front-end application using React and Flask.

4. **Evaluation**:

   - Measured success based on user satisfaction and iteration speed.

5. **Ethical Safeguards**:

   - Implemented logging and review mechanisms to monitor misuse.

- **Outcomes**:

    - Reduced design turnaround time by 70%.

    - Increased user engagement, with 85% of clients using the app for iterative design.

    - Successfully aligned output styles with diverse client branding requirements.